# From My Heart

# To Yours

*Love Letters From A Loving Father*

**Dr. Jamie T. Pleasant; Ph.D.**

# From My Heart

# To Yours

***Love Letters From A Loving Father***

**Dr. Jamie T. Pleasant; Ph.D.**

**From My Heart To Yours: Love Letters From A Loving Father**

Copyright © 2013 by Dr. Jamie T. Pleasant; Ph.D.

Biblion Publishing LLC

All rights reserved. No portion of this book may be reproduced, stored in a retrieval system or transmitted in any form or by any means — electronic, mechanical, photocopy, recording or other without the prior written authorization of the author — except for a brief quotation in printed reviews.

Unless otherwise indicated, scripture quotations are from the Holy Bible, New International Version.

**First Edition / First Printing**

ISBN-978-098437487-8

# Table of Contents

| | | |
|---|---|---|
| Letter 1 | I Want You, To Want Me | 15 |
| Letter 2 | This Is How Much I Love You | 23 |
| Letter 3 | Why Don't You Trust Me? | 29 |
| Letter 4 | What Happened To Us? | 35 |
| Letter 5 | I've Got Big Plans For You! | 43 |
| Letter 6 | I Am Right Beside You | 49 |
| Letter 7 | I Really Care About You! | 55 |
| Letter 8 | Wait on Me, I am Working On Your Blessing! | 63 |
| Letter 9 | I Know You Don't Understand | 71 |
| Letter 10 | Get Real With Me! | 79 |
| Letter 11 | Let Me Show You All Of Me | 87 |
| Letter 12 | When You Hurt, I Hurt | 95 |
| Letter 13 | Let's Celebrate! | 103 |
| Letter 14 | If I Say It, It's Done! | 111 |
| Letter 15 | Take A Chance With Me! | 119 |
| Letter 16 | I Specialize In The Impossible | 127 |

# From My Heart To Yours!

Are you ready to experience a closer relationship with God? Do you want to hear His voice and listen to the great things that He wants to share with you? Are you tired of living each day not really knowing how God feels or cares about you? If you answered yes to any of these questions, this book is for you! "From My Heart to Yours" will take you on a journey to uncovering the promises and speaking words of God. Each chapter presents a personal love letter from a loving Father that will pull you into a more intimate relationship with Him. You will reach new heights in your personal walk with Him as well! You will learn new ways to make decisions. You will walk in a newness of confidence and joy. Get ready to hear His heart speak to yours!

# Dedication

To my daddy, Anthony T. Pleasant, who was a perfect example to me of a real man. To my wife Kimberly (oh, how I love you darling!), my two sons; Christian and Zion, and daughter, Nacara.

To the New Zion Christian Church Family, Dexter Davis, Randy Anderson, Louis Fleming, Brian Simmons, Morgan Fouch-Brooks (my favorite student of all time), Mrs. Julia Ann Pleasant, Jennifer Ford (thanks for being a great friend) and to the late Mrs. Barbara Ann Fouch-Roseboro. Barbara, you taught me how to do business! I will never forget the times we spent together. You always displayed great class and style! Rest easy in His bosom. I love you dearly.

Humbly Yours in Christ,

Apostle Jamie T. Pleasant

# Getting the most out of "From My Heart To Yours"

Congratulations on purchasing this book! Get ready to take your life to a new level. This book includes 16 love-filled letters of God expressing Himself personally to you in a very intimate way. You can use this book for personal growth or group study sessions. All of the scriptures are from the New International Version (1984), or NIV Bible translation (unless otherwise noted). Each day, you will find a unique love letter from God to you that will deeply touch you as He reveals Himself to you like He has never before. Sit back and relax as you listen to Him pour out His love, "From His Heart to Yours"!

## Love Letter 1

## *I Want You To Want Me*

**Psalm 23:1-2 (NIV)**
**[1] The LORD is my shepherd, I shall not be in want. [2] He makes me lie down in green pastures, he leads me beside quiet waters,**

**Dear Restless One:**

I want you to know that there will be times when you will find yourself in uncomfortable situations, where you will become very uneasy and unstable. I want you to allow me to take control of your life and guide you into a peaceful place where you will find rest for your soul. Look at how I ministered to David. He was one of my most loyal servants and sometimes he would find himself in very uncomfortable situations. I don't want you to be too hard on yourself when you are experiencing difficult times in your life. What I want you to do, is put your trust in me to guide you to a quiet place when everything around you seems to be falling apart. I want you to desire to be with me and to allow me to listen to your needs and wants and provide for you. Will you let me do that? I desire to show you how much I want you, to want me. I need your love as much as you need mine. I want you to learn what David learned, and that was, when things get out of control and become nerve-wrecking, call on me and ask me to guide you to a peaceful and quiet place. I am the good shepherd and I know when you need to rest and when you need to get back into the everyday responsibilities of life. I want you to learn how to enjoy the journey so that you can prosper in the fullness of your blessing when you get to your destiny. I ask you and beg you to let me guide all aspects of your life. Let me take you to a place where nothing can harm you or hurt you. Let me take you to a place where there are no worries. Let me take you to a place where you don't have to try to keep up with someone or compete with anyone. Let me take you to a place where you can take a deep breath and exhale all the concerns of your life. Doesn't that sound great? I thought it would. Remember loved one, I will never leave you or forsake you. I want to show you how much I love you by showing you the very best and peaceful time you could ever have in your life. I want to be more than a shepherd to you. I want to be your friend. I want you to know that you are loved. I want you to know that I care for you. Come on, take my hand and let me lead you to a beautiful and peaceful place. Let me take you to paradise. Close your eyes, reach out your hand and wait for my touch. If you wait for a few seconds, you will feel the sensation of warmth in your hand. When you do, that will be me connecting with you. I will be connecting with

*I Want You To Want Me*

your deepest joys, hurts, doubts and anything else that you may be experiencing. However, I don't want you to miss the most important thing here. When we connect, you will experience my peace, love, joy, understanding and power on a new level. When all of me connects with all of you, eternity will unfold itself into a beautiful bouquet of flowers that can't do anything but be admired and appreciated by all that watch the unfolding of our love for each other. Come on, let's go on a beautiful journey together beside the still and peaceful waters.

Yours Forever,

Jehovah-Shalom
The Lord is your peace (Isaiah 9:6)

---

Write your response to what you are feeling right now.

---

## *I Want You To Want Me*

_____

_____

_____

_____

_____

_____

_____

What will you do from now on when you are facing un-nerving situations in your life?

_____

_____

_____

_____

What should you do when you feel like God is reaching out to you and longs to make a connection in time with you?

What circumstance(s) have you faced in the past where you ran away from God rather than allowing Him to lead you to a better place where you would find peace?

_____

_____

_____

_____

_____

_____

How did you overcome your concerns and rested in His love for you that he wanted to show you?

_____

_____

*I Want You To Want Me*

# Love Letter 2

## *This Is How Much I Love You*

**Romans 8:38-39 (NIV)**
**For I am convinced that neither death nor life, neither angels nor demons, neither the present nor the future, nor any powers, neither height nor depth, nor anything else in all creation, <u>*will be able to separate us from the love of God*</u> that is in Christ Jesus our Lord.**

**Dear Beloved Child:**

Do you have any idea how much I love you? Do you know how much you mean to me? Look at what I told Paul to say to remind you of my love for you. Nothing can come between you and me. I am a loving Father and want you to know that I will not fall out of love with you. In fact, there is no evil principality, power, demon or even angel that can whisper in my ear or falsely accuse you and change my feelings about you. I loved you, before you loved yourself. I loved you, before you knew what love was. Why would I let someone come between us? I can't do that. It is not my nature. Stop doubting my love for you. When you fail, don't run and hide from me. Don't think that I will not listen to you or never give you another chance. Trust me and love me back. Let me know how much you love me. Write me a poem. Sing to me. Write me a letter. Talk to me when you are down. Let me know what is on your mind. I won't turn my back on you. I will listen to you and express my love to you. I am a loving Father that forgives and loves unconditionally. Nothing can separate me from you, based on how strongly I feel about you. Stop looking at me only as a God that rules over everything. Start seeing me as your Father. See me as a loving, forgiving,

## *This Is How Much I Love You*

understanding and patient Daddy. That's who I am. That is who I want to become for you. I love you precious child. I really do. I love you with all my heart!

Your Daddy,

Jehovah-Eli
The Lord your God (Psalm 18:2)


Write your response to what you are feeling right now.

_____

_____

_____

_____

_____

_____

*This Is How Much I Love You*

What can you do to make sure you never forget how much God loves you?

_____

_____

_____

_____

_____

_____

_____

_____

_____

***This Is How Much I Love You***

What can you do to remind God that you love him?

_____

_____

_____

_____

_____

_____

_____

_____

_____

_____

What does love mean to you?

## *This Is How Much I Love You*

# Love Letter 3

# Why Don't You Trust Me?

**Proverbs 3:5-6 (NIV)**
**⁵ Trust in the Lord with all your heart and lean not on your own understanding;**
**⁶ in all your ways acknowledge him, and he will make your paths straight.**

**Dearest One:**

You have no idea how I long for you to place all of your trust in me. I watch you as you try to go about your way doing things without asking me for help. I watch you struggle and experience setback after setback, because you have done something on your own without my guidance. How I wish you would bring your concerns and

## *Why Don't You Trust Me?*

plans to me and let me advise and direct your steps. I have been around much longer than you have. I have seen more than you will ever see. I have even experienced more than you could ever experience. So, why do you continue to do things on your own without me beside you to make your path successful? What can I do to earn your trust? Why can't you get real with me and pour your heart out to me with all of your concerns? Do you love me? Do you think I am old fashioned and have no place in your life? Do you still need me? Or, is it that I am not useful to you anymore? Well, your actions show me that you don't trust me. When you make a decision by yourself, it hurts me. It hurts me when I watch you do things that are not beneficial to your well-being. It hurts me because I know it will set you back. It hurts me because I know you will become frustrated. I remember how I was hurt when Adam and Eve chose to taste the fruit from the forbidden tree. I talked to them and told them what was best for them. They did not pay any attention to me and made a decision based on how they felt and the way they saw things. They thought they really didn't need to consult me, and look at what happened. They thought that their knowledge and understanding was enough, and that they didn't need my guidance or blessing. They were wrong and it took me a long time to make things right again. See, dear one, I want the best for you. I don't want to hold you back. I don't want to hold you down. I simply want the best for you. However, you have to trust me. You have to lean on me and not yourself. I birthed you to be able to show you how much I really care. Please, just trust me.

Love Always,

Jehovah-Rohi
The Lord your Shepherd (Psalm 23)

## *Why Don't You Trust Me?*

Write your response to what you are feeling right now.

_____

_____

_____

_____

What can you do to make sure you never forget to include God in your plans?

_____

_____

_____

_____

_____

## *Why Don't You Trust Me?*

_____

What can you do to show God that you trust him?

_____

_____

_____

_____

_____

_____

What does trust mean to you?

_____

_____

_____

_____

*Why Don't You Trust Me?*

# Love Letter 4

# What Happened To Us?

**Deuteronomy 31:8 (NIV)**
**[8]...he will never leave you nor forsake you...**

**My Love:**

What happened to us? I remember when we first met, and how you came to me with open arms. With love, you expressed your most inner thoughts to me. You would tell me any and everything. Do you remember how we used to chat, laugh and walk together? You couldn't wait to wake up and express your thoughts to me. You were not able to stay away from my house, especially on Sundays. You came early and stayed

## What Happened To Us?

late. You would get excited and sometimes even dance with me. Now, you come around every now and then. You act as though you never knew me. You would hold my hand and proudly tell people how you felt and enjoyed my touch. Now, you seem so far away. It's as if we never had a relationship with each other. What happened to us? What went wrong? Tell me. I want to know because I want to change things. I want us to get back to where we used to be. Back in love. Back in peace. Back in joy. Where did those days go? I want them back again. See, child, I miss you. I need you in my life. I need to see your smiling face. I need to hold your hand. **I NEED YOU DESPERATELY!** Come back to me and I will welcome you. I remember how the Israelites left me and abandoned me for another. They forgot all about me. They put me on the back burner for a quick thrill that only lasted a short time. They forgot that I made them who they were. I chose to prosper them. I created them to be set apart from

## *What Happened To Us?*

all others on Earth for my pleasure. I was hurt when they walked away from me. Oh, how they hurt me. They really hurt me to the core. However, I am faithful, I am forgiving, and I still love them. Likewise, I have an everlasting love for you that can't be defined by any known dictionary. I have a love for you that will outlast time. I have a love for you that can't be compared to any living and breathing thing on this Earth. Give me another chance. Let me come back into your life. I am a loving Father that wants to show His love to you. Child of mine, I love you very much. I will never leave you or forsake you. I have an everlasting love for you that will never end. I am faithful when it comes to you. I just want you back. I want you to love me with all your heart. Will you come back to me?

Yours Truly,

Jehovah-Sel'i
The Lord your Rock (Psalm 18:2)

## *What Happened To Us?*

Write your response to what you are feeling right now.

_____

_____

_____

_____

_____

_____

_____

_____

_____

_____

## What Happened To Us?

What can you do to make sure God never feels like you turned your back on Him?

*What Happened To Us?*

_____

_____

_____

What can you do to show that you are committed to God?

_____

_____

_____

_____

_____

_____

_____

## *What Happened To Us?*

_____

_____

_____

_____

What is the difference in saying you love someone and showing him or her that you love them?

_____

_____

_____

_____

_____

_____

_____

*What Happened To Us?*

## Love Letter 5

# I've Got Big Plans For You!

**Jeremiah 29:11 (NIV)**
**[11] For I know the plans I have for you," declares the LORD, "plans to prosper you and not to harm you, plans to give you hope and a future.**

**Cherished One:**

I just want to write you a note to let you know that you are on my mind. I want you to know that I have some big plans for you. I want to make sure that you become everything that I ever intended you to be. You see, from the beginning of time, I had plans for all of my children. None of my children are the same. However, I have given each

## *I've Got Big Plans For You!*

of my children special abilities and gifts to operate in blessings, while fulfilling their purpose on this Earth. I want you to know that my plans will prosper you and make you better. I take no joy in holding you back or seeing you suffer. All I ask of you is that you seek me and then follow my directions to the letter in order to walk in your prosperity. If you remember, I had plans for Abraham to become a great nation. Do you remember that? I told him in order to be blessed from all corners of the Earth, he had to leave his familiar surroundings and follow the path I would lay down for him daily. At first, he had some problems doing that. However, he soon got the hang of it and I was able to bless every single thing he touched. In order for you to be blessed, you must follow me and all the plans I lay out for you. You can't veer to the right or the left. You must stay on the straight course that I lay out for you. Please know that I don't prosper my loved ones in a way that one would expect. No! I

## *I've Got Big Plans For You!*

usually bless and prosper in situations that seem disastrous and harmful to the human mind and eye. Listen closely; I want to share a big secret with you, my special one. The path may look like it is harmful. The path may look treacherous. The path may even look destructive. However, the truth is, my plan will provide prosperity and blessings for you if you keep your feet firm and true to what I called you to do. Simply put, I want to make sure you trust me and my plans more than you fear people and their doubts. Yes, child of mine, I have big plans for you. Plans that you can't even imagine. Plans that you won't understand. Nevertheless, I will make sure to do all I can, to get you to walk in your blessings. I love you just that much. Now, would you please relax and let me birth my plans in you? I really have the best for you, ok? I can't wait to talk to you again soon.

## *I've Got Big Plans For You!*

Your loving Dad,

Jehovah-M'Kaddesh
The Lord your Sanctifier (1 Corinthians 1:30)

Write your response to what you are feeling right now.

_____

_____

_____

_____

_____

_____

_____

_____

## *I've Got Big Plans For You!*

What can you do to make sure you never miss God's plans?

_____

_____

_____

_____

_____

What can you do to stay on the path God has laid out for you?

_____

_____

_____

_____

*I've Got Big Plans For You!*

What does the word *"plan"* mean to you?

## Love Letter 6

# I Am Right Beside You

**Daniel 3:25 (NIV)**
**25 He said, "Look! I see four men walking around in the fire, unbound and unharmed, and the fourth looks like a son of the gods."**

**Precious One:**

I was thinking of you and wanted you to know that you are never alone. I am always with you in tight spots that may make you feel uncomfortable. I want you to think back at how I helped the three Hebrew boys when they were in the fiery furnace. I love showing up in these kinds of circumstances. It was very hot in the furnace but I knew they could handle it. Did you notice how I had my Son right beside them and how He never left their side? Did you see how I kept them from catching on fire? Did you notice that they didn't even smell like smoke when they came out? Guess what? I want to do the same thing for you. I want to do more than tell you that you are blessed. I want to do more than tell you that you are more than a conqueror. I want to get in the fire right beside you. I want to stand with you. I want your enemies to look in and see that the hand of God is on you and nothing that they can do can ever harm you because of my strong love for you. Oh Yeah! I have a love for you that no flame can destroy, no demon can come between and no hater can stop. I am always with you and will never leave you as I stand with you in the middle of your trial. Now, isn't that good news? You are a child of a strong Father! I am a powerful Father! No one can mess with my child and not have to answer to me. I am always on time and full of power when I show up! So, let's go do something great together! Let's make a stand together! Let's make history together! I am with you and got your back!

Sincerely Yours,

Jehovah-'Immeku
The Lord that is with you (Judges 6:12)


Write your response to what you are feeling right now.

_____

_____

_____

_____

_____

_____

## *I Am Right Beside You*

_____

What can you do to be assured that God is with you always?

_____

_____

_____

_____

_____

What should you do when facing uncomfortable situations when you feel all alone?

_____

_____

_____

## *I Am Right Beside You*

_____

_____

_____

_____

What circumstance have you faced in the past that made you wonder if God was with you?

_____

_____

_____

_____

_____

_____

_____

_____

## *I Am Right Beside You*

## Love Letter 7

# I Really Care About You!

**Mark 4:38 (KJV)**
[38]……Master, carest thou not that we perish?

**Dear Love:**

Never doubt my love for you! I love you more than you will ever know. I know there are times when it seems like I am not around. However, I am always just a call away from you. I remember how I had the disciples on the boat with my Son on their way to the other side of the sea. I remember how He had a plan to teach them that they should never worry about anything as long as they knew that He was right beside them. I wanted them to know that when He invites someone to do something, there is nothing that can stop or destroy the plan He has already put in motion. I want you to understand that when I start something in your life, don't let distractions or sudden storms scare or stop you from going in the direction I am taking you. Loved one, if you will notice, they started asking Him if He really cared about them. They were wondering if He had planned their demise. I tell you, He had a plan. He already knew what He wanted to do. He simply wanted them to learn how to act the way He would act when unexpected negative events might come up. I want you to notice where He was when the storm broke out. He was at the back of the boat sleeping. He was in the back of the boat in a blissful state of rest and peace. I want you to learn from this that you should never let a storm take you out of your blissful peace and state of rest where I have placed you. If I have asked you to do something, when a storm breaks out, rest! If I have commissioned you to complete an assignment, when a storm breaks out, rest! If I have called you to let me use you to build my kingdom while serving in your purpose, when a storm breaks out, rest! Never let a storm take you out of your blessing! Never! Notice how He awakened and commanded the wind and the sea to quiet down and be still. I want you to do what He did. Quiet your storm and command it to be still and remain peaceful. Tell your storm that you are a child of God. Let your storm know that I am with you and that you have authority. Let your storm know that you have been commissioned to change the atmosphere. Let your storm know that you can change it, but it can't change you! Tell it to take a back seat to what I am doing in your life! Tell it to go somewhere else. Let it know that you have too much power and too many blessings where you are right now with me! I want you to walk as I walk. I want you to do as I do. I want you to be as I am. Remember; don't just ask what

## *I Really Care About You!*

I would do. On the contrary, do what I am doing. Walk and act like the powerful person I created you to be. Become a victor! Become a champion! Become an overcomer! I care about you and never want you to doubt that truth. If you trust me and call to me, I will always deliver and bless you. I really will. There may be times that you think I am not around. There may be times that you think I am too busy doing other things. There may be times you may think I have other things on my mind. That is far from the truth. I am just relaxing in peace, preparing a plan for your deliverance. Isn't that awesome? Trust me; I really care about you, my precious jewel.

Yours Truly,

Jehovah-Shammah
The Lord of the Present (Hebrews 13:5)


Write your response to what you are feeling right now.

## *I Really Care About You!*

Do you now have confidence that God cares about you? Explain, why or why not.

## I Really Care About You!

_____

_____

What should you do when you feel like God doesn't care about your present condition?

_____

_____

_____

_____

_____

_____

What circumstance have you faced in the past that made you wonder if God really cared about you?

_____

## *I Really Care About You!*

_____

_____

_____

_____

_____

How did you overcome those doubts and rest in His peace knowing He had a plan for your deliverance?

_____

_____

_____

_____

_____

## *I Really Care About You!*

## Love Letter 8

# Wait On Me, I Am Working On Your Blessing!

**Isaiah 40:31 (KJV)**
**³¹ But they that wait upon the LORD shall renew *their* strength; they shall mount up with wings as eagles; they shall run, and not be weary; *and* they shall walk, and not faint.**

**Dear Child:**

I know that it's hard to wait on me. I understand that sometimes you want me to move and act as fast as possible. However, I want you to know that when it feels like I am not moving fast enough for you, I am actually working in the background on a blessing for you that you can't even see. Do you remember the time when you needed some money and it seemed like it was never going to come? Well, I want you to know that I was working overtime for you in the background making sure you wouldn't lose the stuff that you had, that the enemy was trying to take from you. Yes! I was making sure that the basic things you always had, would not be stolen by the evil one. I remember when you asked me for some money to get something. I knew you needed the money as soon as possible. I knew you had to have it or things wouldn't work out. However, I had to make sure that while you were seeking money for that one thing, you weren't going to lose the most important things that you needed to sustain your life. Do you know that one time the evil one wanted to place cancer in your body and I had to work overtime to fight it and keep you healthy? I knew that all of the money in the world wouldn't mean anything to you if you had been diagnosed with cancer. I had to direct all of my healing power and love towards your body, in order for you to be healed. See, I am always working out a blessing in your life, even when it doesn't seem that way. Notice, how I made sure that the Prophet Isaiah would come to understand that if he would just wait on me and never quit hoping in me, I would come in his life and give him a newness of mind, body and spirit. I knew that this would place him in a position to be victorious at just the right time. Waiting on me, means that I am working out your blessing so that at just the right time, you will have all the strength and energy you need to enjoy and keep the blessing I give to you. See, I want you to enjoy my blessings and not be worn out or over burdened with them. I want you to know that the key to blessings in this life is not just getting things that you want, but wanting them, and keeping them, after you get them! Yes! You have to pace yourself when it

## *Wait On Me, I Am Working On Your Blessing!*

comes to my blessings! You have to know how to enjoy the different seasons of anticipation, contemplation, preparation and celebration. These seasons are part of my plan to develop your character, spirit and mind so that you can experience all of the joy that I want you to have in this life from me. So, please take the time and wait on me. Wait for me to give you the strength to keep your blessings! Wait for me to give you the joy so that you can bask in your blessings! Yes, wait for me, and you will never go wrong. I always know what you need at just the right time. I love you.

With all my love,

Jehovah Jireh
The Lord your Provider (Gen. 22:14)


Write your response to what you are feeling right now.

## *Wait On Me, I Am Working On Your Blessing!*

_____

_____

_____

_____

_____

What type of attitude will you have from now on when you have to wait for God?

_____

_____

_____

_____

_____

_____

_____

## *Wait On Me, I Am Working On Your Blessing!*

What should you do when you feel like God is taking too long to answer you or do something for you?

_____

_____

_____

_____

_____

_____

What circumstance(s) have you faced in the past that made you wonder if God was ignoring you and had other things to do that were more important than what you were dealing with?

_____

## *Wait On Me, I Am Working On Your Blessing!*

_____

_____

_____

_____

_____

How did you overcome those concerns and rested in His promise that He was working in the background on a blessing for you?

_____

_____

_____

_____

_____

## *Wait On Me, I Am Working On Your Blessing!*

_____

_____

_____

_____

_____

# Love Letter 9

# I Know You Don't Understand

**Isaiah 55:8 (NIV)**
**"For my thoughts are not your thoughts, neither are your ways my ways," declares the LORD.**

**Genesis 3:6 (NIV)**
**When the woman saw that the fruit of the tree <u>*was good*</u> for food and pleasing to the eye, and also desirable for gaining wisdom, she took some and ate it. She also gave some to her husband, who was with her, and he ate it.**

**Dear Loved One:**

I know that there are things that might be happening in your life that you don't understand.

## *I Know You Don't Understand*

You might be wondering why you didn't get that job that you really wanted. You might be wondering why you were not invited to that event you really wanted to go to. You might be wondering why someone that you thought was a friend, turned their back on you and no longer talks to you. You might even be wondering if you are a good parent, spouse or friend to those that you care about. There are many things that don't make sense to you sometimes, I know. However, I want you to know that I watched all of these things as they were happening to you. The reason I allowed all of these things to happen to you, was to give you the very best of what I have for you and not just things you think, are good for you. There is a difference among "good things" and "best things". "Good things" bring temporary happiness to you. "Good things" don't bring the long-term fulfillment that I want you to have in your life. "Good things" will never satisfy your inner being. However, my "best things" will bring long term joy to you. My "best things" will satisfy you on a level like you have never experienced before. My "best things" will satisfy your inner being for all of eternity. The next time things don't seem to work out your way, know that I have a "best plan" for your life. I want to give you my best. I want you to have the best of everything. You don't need a "good man" or "good woman", you need a "best man" or "best woman". Don't settle for second bests or leftovers. Wait on the best that I have for you. Remember that in this life, there are many "good trees" that you can pick "good things" from. However, there is a tree that has all the "best things" that I have prepared for you. Wait and be patient and pick from the best. When you pick from the best, you will always pick a winner! You will always pick a blessing! You will always pick my desire for you. Now, my child, go and pick from the tree of life that which is the best for you. Walk in peace and joy everyday of your life! I love you.

## *I Know You Don't Understand*

Yours Forever,

Jehovah Jireh
The Lord your Provider (1 John 4:9)

Write your response to what you are feeling right now.

_____

_____

_____

_____

_____

_____

_____

Were there times when you wondered what God was doing as you were turned down for that "good thing" in your life? If so, write below how you dealt with it.

_____

_____

_____

_____

_____

_____

How will you deal with having to wait for God's best in the future?

_____

_____

_____

What negative circumstance(s) have you faced in the past that made you wonder if God was playing games with you or getting you back for something you had done wrong?

## *I Know You Don't Understand*

_____

_____

How did you overcome those concerns and waited for His best in your life. Write on one side of this paper on the lines, the "good thing(s)" that you wanted that you didn't get. Write on the other side the "best thing(s)" that he gave to you instead.

| Good Things | Best Things |
|---|---|
|   |   |
|   |   |
|   |   |
|   |   |
|   |   |
|   |   |
|   |   |

## *I Know You Don't Understand*

# Love Letter 10

# Get Real With Me!

**1 Peter 5:7 (NIV)**
**⁷ Cast all your anxiety on him because he cares for you.**

**Dear Fearful One:**

Why are you afraid of me? Why can't you tell me the truth about all that you are dealing with and going through? Why are you embarrassed to share your deepest, darkest secrets, fears and concerns with me? Do you think I will love you less? Do you think I will walk away from you? I know, you think I will not look at you the same way after you open up to me and tell me everything. Listen to me, I know everything about you. I know more about you than you know about yourself. I know what you are going to do, before you do it. Ask

*Get Real With Me!*

Peter. My Son told him that he would deny Him three times and he swore he wouldn't do it, but he did. Yet, he was forgiven. I will forgive you too. I want you to know that I don't want you to be anxious when you come to me and tell me what you are dealing with. I also want you to know, that when you are anxious, you are walking in fear. You must know that you can't expect to get relief from your problems, issues and concerns, if you don't honestly cast all of your cares on my Son Jesus. You can't tell Him about half of your issues. You have to tell Him about everything you are dealing with. Don't expect to get relief from a bill if you don't tell Him the entire truth about how the bill came to be. Tell Him about the role you played in making it difficult for you to pay that bill. Don't tell Him about half of it, tell my Son about all of it! All I want you to do is be real with me by telling my Son everything. Don't hold anything back. Open up your heart to Him and dump it all out into His loving hands. Neither He nor I will walk away from you. I will open up my heart to you and give you strength and courage to face your issues and concerns. I love those that are real with me and not afraid to tell me the truth about themselves. If you are a liar, tell me. I'll still love you. If you are a cheat, tell me. I will still love you. If you are a thief, tell me. I will still love you. In fact, the more truthful you are with me, the more I will show you my love. You can always come to me and tell me your deepest concerns. I love real people. My Son, Jesus told Peter that he would deny Him three times, and he did. After Peter denied him, my Son looked for him, found him and forgave him. He then made him the first leader of the church in this world. Now if I can forgive and use him, you had better believe I can forgive and use you. Once I forgive you, I will no longer remember your sins, failures or faults. Come on, open up to me right now and share your most intimate thoughts with me. Share your bad thoughts with me as well. Tell me about all of the bad things that exist in your life. I can take it. I am God. I am here for you for all of eternity. I just want you to be real. That's real talk, from a real God.

Forever Forgiven,

Jehovah-Chatsahi
The Lord is Your Strength (Psalm 27:1)

Write your response to what you are feeling right now.

_____

_____

_____

_____

_____

_____

## Get Real With Me!

_____

How will you approach God now when you are troubled or in a trying situation and seeking relief?

_____

_____

_____

_____

_____

_____

What should you do when you feel like God will not love you as much as He did before if you do something displeasing to Him?

_____

What circumstance(s) have you faced in the past that made you wonder that if you really told God the truth, He would distance Himself from you?

How will you make sure you never stop telling God the truth about certain things that are embarrassing to you?

*Get Real With Me!*

## Love Letter 11

# Let Me Show You All Of Me

**Psalm 119:130 (NIV)**
**130 The unfolding of your words gives light; it gives understanding to the simple.**

**Dear Curious One:**

Have you ever desired to get to know me on a more personal and intimate level? Do you want to know what gets me excited? Have you ever thought about the things that make me happy? Well, I want to share some things with you that I haven't shared with many. I want you to know the most intricate details about me. Are you ready? Ok. Here it goes. I am a God that loves to be loved. I am a God that loves to be in relationship with his people. I am a God that is looking for someone that is willing to partner with me in establishing my Son's kingdom on Earth. I am a God that wants to help you obtain every blessing I have ever planned for you. Many wonder what is required to get to know me better. Well, I am ready to share a secret with you. All you have to do is take time and begin to seek me through the word. That is, the Bible. Now hold on a minute. I want you to open the Bible and begin reading some passages of scripture. Watch and see, if I will not become a living reality to you. You can start anywhere in the bible that you like. I strongly suggest that you isolate yourself so that you will not be easily distracted. Every day I want you to set aside a certain time to meet with me through the written word. Now it will take a few moments, but, watch and see if after a little while you begin to experience a calmness and peace like you never have before. Watch and see if all of a sudden you start coming up with solutions to the problems you may be facing. Watch and see if you will not start

## *Let Me Show You All Of Me*

dreaming dreams in the middle of reading scripture like you never have before. You will even begin to think thoughts that you never thought of before. Do you know what is happening when you begin to experience these things? I am revealing myself to you; so that you can see all the things, I designed you to do before you were ever born. You will never realize your true purpose in life until you become one with me and I with you. I want to show you all of me and become one with you, so that you can become an outward expression of my inner desires. That's right! I designed you to become a living reality of who I am. I want people to see with their natural eyes the greatness that I have placed inside of you. When they see your greatness, it is just my greatness expressed through you, in human form. That is something to think about isn't it? I know it is. Now, you can't just come to me for a quick moment and expect to walk away with all the essence of who I am. You will have to spend time with me to be able to become a full expression of my love. In fact, I very seldom show my inner self to those that don't have time to patiently wait until I can reveal the fullness of their destiny in time and space. Curious One, I want you to understand that you are like a rose petal that opens gradually over time. No one can fully appreciate a rose's beauty until it reaches full blossom. That is the same way it is when I am revealing myself to you. Each day, I will slowly reveal portions of myself to you, until one day, you look up and find yourself being admired by all, to see the fullness of your beauty. They will see all of my fullness expressed through you when they see your peace! They will see my fullness expressed through you when they see your joy! They will see my fullness expressed through you, when they see all of your great accomplishments. I want to show you all of me, so you can show this world of doubters all of you as an outward expression of all of me. It can only happen through the unfolding of time. It can only happen through the unfolding of knowledge. It can only happen through the unfolding of my love. It can only happen through the unfolding of my word being read and applied daily in your life. So, what are you waiting for? Go get the Bible and we can begin this journey together. Let me show you all of me. I love you so much. Take care, Curious One.

Yours in love,

Jehovah-Bara
The Lord your Creator (Isaiah 40:28)

Write your response to what you are feeling right now.

_____

_____

_____

_____

How will you approach God now when you feel like getting closer to Him or knowing Him better?

What should you do when you feel like God is distancing Himself from you?

What can you do more of in your Bible time to make sure you connect with God and become one with Him?

## *Let Me Show You All Of Me*

How will you make sure you never miss God's presence and precious moments that He wants to spend with you to share more of Himself?

_____

_____

_____

_____

_____

_____

_____

_____

_____

_____

## Love Letter 12

# When You Hurt,

# I Hurt

**John 11:33-36 (NIV)**
**[33] When Jesus saw her weeping, and the Jews who had come along with her also weeping, he was deeply moved in spirit and troubled.**
**[34] "Where have you laid him?" he asked.**
**"Come and see, Lord," they replied.**
**[35] Jesus wept.**
**[36] Then the Jews said, "See how he loved him!"**

**To My Most Loved One:**

I want you to know, that when you hurt, I hurt also. Look at how my son, Jesus responded to Lazarus being dead. Look at how He felt the pain of Mary, Lazarus' sister. Always know that I feel what you feel. Believe me, when I feel what you feel, I will do something about it. I take no pleasure in watching you go through hurt and pain. I wish you would never have to experience such things. However, as life is full of sin and negative events, there will be times when you will hurt. Do you remember when your heart was broken because of your breakup with your mate? Do you remember the time when you felt bad because you didn't get that job, degree, car, home or promotion you wanted? I remember those times. I was right there looking at you to the point that I became troubled and hurt just like you did. You cried, and I did too. You felt bad, and I did too. You were miserable, and I was miserable too. Did you ever wonder why I didn't immediately come to your rescue? Well, the simple answer is, I had to let destiny take its course. There are times when unfortunate events will occur in your life and I must stand back and let them happen. Please understand I will not allow anything to happen to you that will make your life worst in the end or jeopardize your walk with me. There are times unfortunate things will occur that will cause you to cry and want to quit life. Please know that I am experiencing these things along with you in order to get you to a better place in your life. Your destination will be better than you ever imagined and this may be the only way to get you there. Yes, my loved one, even when you lose a person close to you in death, I am working on something better to happen to you. Mary and her sister Martha had to experience their brother's death, in order to see a bigger miracle, which was his resurrection. Now, I know that you might have loved ones that have died and are still dead. However, I want you to know even though they may have died, something or someone was definitely resurrected! There is no death that does not produce a resurrection! At every funeral, someone is touched by death and will focus on me and begin to direct their lives according to my will. You see, what Jesus was showing Mary and

Martha was that unless a seed falls to the ground, there is no chance for another life to grow. I want you to think a moment about a loved one close to you that has died. Now, think about how you or someone you know, changed their lives significantly after that. Often, this is how death works through people. Notice that Mary and Martha became very strong in their faith and love for Christ. Notice also, how all of the people watching saw how much my Son really loved Lazarus, by giving him the ability to live again. What a beautiful thing the effects of that one death brought to that city. Please remember, there will be times when troubling situations occur in your life, but be assured that I am right beside you sharing in your pain and trouble. Never forget that I will provide a way of relief to come out of all your trying times. In the future, promise me that you will share all of your hurts with me. Tell Me everything, so that I can become closer to you than you could ever imagine. I want to share in your

## *When You Hurt, I Hurt*

trials, so I can better celebrate with you in your triumphs! So, let's do this together. Let's walk through the fire, rain and sunshine together. I am an all weather God. I am with you through it all. I will never leave you, nor forsake you. I promise. I love you.

Yours in Peace,

Jehovah Shalom
The Lord of Peace (Rom 8:31-35)

Write your response to what you are feeling right now.

_____

_____

_____

_____

_____

*When You Hurt, I Hurt*

_____

_____

How will you approach God now when you feel troubled and confused about why unfortunate things are happening to you?

_____

_____

_____

_____

_____

_____

What should you do when you feel like God is not with you in trying times?

## *When You Hurt, I Hurt*

What can you do more of to assure yourself that God feels your pain and is there to help you?

How will you assure God that He is the only One that you trust during trying times and uncomfortable situations?

# Love Letter 13

## *Let's Celebrate!*

**Luke 15:23 (NIV)**
**²³ Bring the fattened calf and kill it. Let's have a feast and celebrate.**

**Dear Reserved One:**

I want you to begin to have more fun! Yes! I said it! I want you to begin to let your hair down, take off your shoes, relax and celebrate. The message I want you to take away from this letter is to learn how to celebrate precious moments in your life and not let them slip away unnoticed. I love to celebrate and want my children to do the same. I really do. Do you remember how I commanded the Israelites to celebrate the Passover, the Feast of Weeks, the Year of Jubilee, the Feast of Unleavened Bread and, let us not forget, the Sabbath? Do you see how I like to celebrate with

## Let's Celebrate!

my children? I want you and I to experience the same good times together as well. Notice in the scripture, how the father reacts to his disobedient son's return home. He doesn't scorn him or make him feel bad. He throws a big celebration to let everyone know that he is glad his son has returned home. I want you to begin to celebrate your mistakes as well. You should always celebrate your life lessons. I don't want you to be so hard on yourself, that you become depressed and disengaged with others that mean so much to you when you fail. All of my children make mistakes. Only when you acknowledge your mistakes and the lessons that you have learned from them, can you be free to throw a big celebration. I want you to celebrate the little things that you take for granted as well. Don't just celebrate birthdays, anniversaries, holidays and graduations. I want you to start having big celebrations every time you get a promotion, earn an "A" on a paper, win a game, and are accepted into a club or organization.

## *Let's Celebrate!*

I want you to celebrate your children. I want you to celebrate when they score their first point or touchdown. Celebrate when they finish their first recital. Celebrate every grade report period when they earn "A's" and "B's". Celebrate! Celebrate when your friend gets a new car, house, clean bill of health or loses weight. Celebrate! Celebrate when you buy your first expensive watch, article of clothing or jewelry. Celebrate! I will be watching to see if you will begin to celebrate life. Also, and most importantly, don't hesitate to celebrate me often! Celebrate me sustaining your life and taking care of you. Celebrate the fact that you have ever-lasting life! Celebrate the truth that you are surrounded with the help of The Father, Son and the Holy Spirit! We are here for you and will help you at all times. Don't be a party pooper. Be the life of the party. In addition, when you celebrate, do it big. Call all of your friends, and let them know that you are celebrating something good that has happened in your life.

## *Let's Celebrate!*

Let them know of my goodness. Tell them about how many times that I have delivered you and sustained you. Tell them how I am always there for you when you need me. Tell them these things when you celebrate. Now, guess what? The most cherished time I love to celebrate with you, is when you come to my church. Yes, that is the best celebration of the week. I love when we can get together and celebrate all the good things that have happened to you. I love when you come to church and share the trying times you have experienced during the week and place your trust in me to take care of them. I love when we get together in church and touch and agree. It is simply the best part of my week. I never miss it. I am always there in the sanctuary waiting on you to find me and come to me in truth and love. What a precious time we always have. By the way, when was the last time that you came to the place where we celebrate? Come on back. Don't be afraid, I'll fatten a cow and serve it up to you. I will have the

## *Let's Celebrate!*

best of everything laid out for you to enjoy. I will even speak to you and tell you about all the great things that are about to happen in your life. Great things that will bring you strength and hope. We will sing some songs, talk to each other and enjoy each other's company. What are you waiting for? Come on back to the house. Come on back to the house of prayer. Come on back to the place where you belong.

Yours and waiting,

Jehovah-Sabaoth
The Lord of Hosts (1 Sam 1:3)

Write your response to what you are feeling right now.

_____

_____

_____

_____

## Let's Celebrate!

How will you approach God when you feel like celebrating?

What should you do when you feel like celebrating small things?

## *Let's Celebrate!*

_____

_____

_____

What can you do more of to assure yourself that you are not missing out on precious moments that you should be celebrating?

_____

_____

_____

_____

_____

How will you make sure that you celebrate the right things to the fullest?

_____

## *Let's Celebrate!*

# Love Letter 14

## *If I Say It,*

## *It's Done!*

**Genesis 1:3 (NIV)**
**³ And God said, "Let there be light," and there was light.**

**Dear Doubtful One:**

I want to let you know that whenever I say something to you, you can count on it happening. What have you heard me say to you lately? Can you even think of one thing? I am constantly trying to get your attention in order to let you know about the plans that I have for you. When I say something, it definitely shall be. Notice how

Moses gives an account of how the Earth began. In the beginning, the earth was formless, empty, dark and without meaning. Pay attention to how I simply speak, and all of a sudden light appears from nowhere. I want to do the same thing in your life. I want to speak into your emptiness and share the fullness of my joy with you. I want to speak into the formless places of your mind, body and spirit to bring structure, purpose and meaning into your life as well. I want to speak into the darkest areas of your life and provide light for you. Do you see what I am trying to do for you? I want to always bring light into your life. Whatever you may be facing, struggling with, or need help with; I am here to speak into your nothing and create something, out of it. Only I can do that. No one else can take a person that is empty and make him/her become full of substance and have meaning, but me. No one else can take a person that can't form anything out of his/her life and make him/her become full of purpose and destiny.

## *If I Say It, It's Done!*

No one can take a person that is dark and filled with evil and shape him/her into a gentle beautiful light that shines into everyone's path to show his/her greatness. No one can do that but me. The more time you spend with me, the more light I will speak into you. You are nothing more than an outward and bright expression of who I am. You truly express yourself to others when your light can shine. I have created every person to uniquely shine in this life. Some will have very bright lights and others will have soft lights that simply compliment their surroundings. Do you know the type of light that you are? In my presence, I will shape you and develop you into the divine light that I always intended you to become. You will go from being sad, to being glad. You will go from being empty, to being full. You will go from being shapeless, into being a mighty person full of substance and purpose. You see, every time that I can speak into your life, you become more alive. Just because you are breathing doesn't mean that you are alive! It is only when you can shine your presence into a dark, empty and meaningless situation, that you are alive. When I speak into your life, no trouble, challenge or uncomfortable situation will get the best of you. Those things will not suck the life out of you anymore. In fact, they will give you life, because you now will be able to shine and show your power and strength. You will thrive on challenges, troubles and trials. So, I ask you, how are you doing? Are you living or just breathing? Are you thriving or dying in your life? Let me speak into your being. Let me speak into your spirit, mind and body. If you will be still and let me speak into your life, you will begin to live a life that is full of the best of everything that you could ever imagine. Remember that my words are spirit and they are life. They give life to those that will allow themselves to be shaped by me. If I can create a universe, I can create your destiny. If I can make a planet out of nothing, I can make you into something that is great. If you look back at Adam, I first imagined him in my mind. I then blew on the dirt and created a small dust storm. I then took my hands and formed him out of dust. However, he was still not alive. I had created him and shaped him, but he did not breathe one single breath. However, when I breathed into his nostrils the breath of life, he became a living soul. Have you not heard that all scripture is God breathed in second Timothy chapter three verse sixteen? Have you ever read that? Well, you should go there and spend some time in my word. Then, you will see that no one can live without scripture breathed into their bodies every day. So, start living and not just existing. Go to my word in the Bible and let me breathe life into you. I want to speak into your life. I want to tell you something that you never thought would happen. I want to show you your future. In addition, remember, if I say it, it will happen. Open up your mouth and nose. Inhale. Now, begin to live. I love you!

## *If I Say It, It's Done!*

Love Always,

Jehovah-Bara
The Lord, your Creator (Isaiah 40:28)

Write your response to what you are feeling right now.

_____

_____

_____

_____

_____

_____

How will you approach God when you are perplexed and or confused?

## *If I Say It, It's Done!*

How will you view yourself when facing challenges from now on?

## *If I Say It, It's Done!*

What can you do to assure yourself that you can handle all uncomfortable and challenging situations in your life?

# Love Letter 15

# Take A Chance With Me!

**Matthew 14:28-29 (NIV)**
[28] "Lord, if it's you," Peter replied, "tell me to come to you on the water." [29] "Come," he said. Then Peter got down out of the boat, walked on the water and came toward Jesus.

**Dear Fearful One:**

I want you to take a chance with me and do something you have never done before. The reason I want you to do something you have never done before, is so I can give you something you've never had before. I want to begin a new adventure with you that will prosper you and elevate you to a new level in life. Look at how I did it with Peter. I always admired him because he was never afraid to take a chance with my Son and me. There are many that associate themselves with me, but never take a chance with me. I have always wondered how someone can say that they are connected with me and yet never do anything radical for me. Did you understand that my child? Do you see what I am saying? I can't understand how someone can be around me all day, pray to me, praise me, claim to know me, and yet, never try to do one supernatural thing in his/her entire life. That is why I chose Peter to be the first leader of my Son's church. I knew he would never be afraid to push the button and do new things in the kingdom for me. What kind of person are you my child? Can I select and trust you to depend on me and get out of your comfort zone of normalcy and do something radical? Will you take a chance with me to change your life? Will you allow me to go ahead of you and prepare a new path for you that will only bring you to a better place, with better things, for a better relationship with me that will yield a better life for you? Will you let me do that? I am waiting on you loved one. If you don't know how to do this, let me help. Just come to me and begin to talk with me and each day I will begin to strengthen you to the point that you will start dreaming new dreams, thinking new thoughts, talking a new talk, walking a new walk and planning new plans. I promise you, that after you start experiencing these things, you will soon find yourself stepping into something new that will change your life. I want you to be watchful of what I am doing in your life. I don't want you to get ahead of me, but to watch me. Did you hear that? Be watchful of me and wait on me to invite you to get out of your normal life so you can step into a new and more powerful life. Be watchful of where I am and what I am doing at all times. Never take your eyes off me. You won't experience all of me unless you

## Take A Chance With Me!

are in constant communication with me and understand all aspects of who I truly am. So, what are you waiting on? What are you afraid of? What's holding you back? Come on, step out on the water, and take on a new adventure to a better life and relationship with me. I want you to accomplish those things you have been fearful of. I want you to have everything that I ever dreamed of you having. Come on, get out of the boat, walk on the water, and get your house, car, healing, confidence, peace, love, forgiveness, boldness, job and everything else you need. I am here waiting for you to take a chance with me.

Love Ya,

Jehovah-Hoshe'ah
The Lord that saves (Psalm 20:9)


Write your response to what you are feeling right now.

***Take A Chance With Me!***

How will you approach God when you feel the urge to leave your comfort zone and do something new?

*Take A Chance With Me!*

How will you make sure you don't get ahead of God when venturing out into something new?

*Take A Chance With Me!*

What can you do to assure yourself that you have the courage and strength to step into a new life with God?

_____

_____

_____

_____

_____

_____

_____

_____

_____

_____

## *Take A Chance With Me!*

## Love Letter 16

# I Specialize In The Impossible

**Daniel 3:22 (NIV)**
**²² The king's command was so urgent and the furnace so hot that the flames of the fire killed the soldiers who took up Shadrach, Meshach and Abednego,**

**Dear Love One:**

I prepared this last letter for you and hope it's a blessing. It is so important, that I had to use the Hebrew boys example again. I want you to know that with me, all things are possible because only I can perform the impossible. I will do miraculous things through you that others will not be able to comprehend. There will be times when you will find yourself in some impossible positions, where it seems like you are not going to make it. Be patient and faithful because I am setting up a scene for everyone to see my ability to deliver you out of a tight situation. The situation might seem hopeless to you, but I have a plan to make you come out smelling like a rose. Those that doubt my abilities will not be able to do anything but bow down and acknowledge me as the Most High God when I deliver you. Besides me, there is truly no other God. I am the Real McCoy. The One and Only. The Real Deal. I am the only God that can bring you into a better place after you were in a trying place. I want you to look at the three Hebrew boys. They were being tested to see if they could stand up for what they believed in. I wanted to test them to see if they would crack under pressure, forget or forsake me. As you know, they didn't show any fear when they were thrown into the fiery furnace. If you read the

## *I Specialize In The Impossible*

scripture in more detail, you will see that the king ordered the furnace's temperature to be turned up seven times hotter than normal. You will also read that the soldiers, who were ordered to turn it up, burned up and died as they were trying to place the three Hebrew boys in the fire. You see, I had already done the impossible, even before they went into the fire. If the soldiers died just by getting next to it, how in the world could the three Hebrew boys survive after being placed in it? Well it is very simple. Please note, that there are some things that I have ordained you to be able to go through, that others can't go through! You see, I have prepared an impossible situation uniquely for you, that only I can make possible for you to go into and come out of, stronger in the end. You will always come out smelling like a rose when you trust me in your time of being tested. Look at how things ended up for them. The king couldn't believe that they hadn't died, so he looked in and did a head count and came up with four people

## *I Specialize In The Impossible*

alive in the furnace. You see, I allowed him to see the revelation of my Son in there with them. I am always beside you working out impossible situations. I am always beside you in your defense. Never, ever, forget that. Whenever you think you are alone, I'm right there! Whenever you think it's over and you won't make it, I'm right there. Whenever you think you are not going to survive, I'm right there. Yes! I am right there making the impossible, possible. Therefore, I have a request of you right now. I wish you would do it for me. I want you to take a second where you are right now and begin to give me praise! I want you to bless me wherever you are right now. Will you give me a shout? Will you lift up your hands? Will you call out my name? I hope you will. If so, it will allow me to enter in your life right now and usher you into a realm of unlimited possibilities. I'm working it out right now! All these things I have written.

## *I Specialize In The Impossible*

From my heart to yours,

Jehovah-'Izoa Hakaboth
The Lord your God, Strong and Mighty (Ps 24:8)

Write your response to what you are feeling right now.

_____

_____

_____

_____

_____

_____

How has this book of love letters from God helped you?

_____

## *I Specialize In The Impossible*

How will you make sure you let God deliver you from trying situations?

*I Specialize In The Impossible*

What can you do to assure yourself that God will never lead you into a hopeless situation without a plan to deliver you?

_____

_____

_____

_____

_____

_____

_____

_____

_____

## *I Specialize In The Impossible*

# Epilogue

One of the best ways to experience the complete love of God in your life is for you to give your life to Christ Jesus. Repeat these simple words and it will be a done deal. Repeat the following: Lord Christ Jesus as of this very moment, I accept you as Lord and Savior of my life. I now give my life to you to be fashioned for your purpose and glory. Lord, all of these things that I have said, I truly believe in my heart and have confessed with my mouth to you. I know now that I have received everlasting life based on the work that Christ has done and will continue to do in my life. Lord Christ, thank you for bringing me to this point of my life where I surrender my all to you. It is in the Holy Spirit through Christ Jesus, I say Amen.

Humbly Yours in Christ

Apostle Jamie T. Pleasant

# *Epilogue*

## *Other Books by Dr. Pleasant*

# For Speaking Engagements

admin@newzionchristianchurch.org or

678.845.7055

These books can be purchased at any bookstore or online at amazon.com, barnesandnoble.com and many other stores and outlets.

## *About the Author*

### ***About the Author***

Apostle Jamie T. Pleasant; Ph.D. is the Chief Executive Pastor and Founder of New Zion Christian Church in Suwanee, Georgia. As a modern day polymath, he holds a bachelor's degree in Physics from Benedict College in Columbia, South Carolina, Marketing Studies from Clemson University and an M.B.A. in Marketing from Clark Atlanta University. On August 13, 1999, Apostle Pleasant achieved a Georgia Tech milestone by becoming the first African American to graduate with a Ph.D. in Business Management in the school's 111 plus year history.

God gave him the vision to establish a Biblically based economic development initiative for New Zion Christian Church. He remains at the pulse of the economic business sector. As a result, Apostle Pleasant is in constant demand to train,

## About the Author

speak and teach others at all levels in ministries and the private sector about business and economic development across the country. He has created cutting edge and industry leading ministerial programs in the church such as The Financial Literacy Academy For Youth (FLAFY), where youth from the ages of 13-19 attend 12 week intense classes on financial money management principles. At the end of 12 weeks, they receive a "Personal Finance" certificate of achievement. Other ministries he has pioneered include; The Wealth Builders Investment Club (WBIC), which educates and allows members to actively invest in the stock market, along with the much celebrated Institute of Entrepreneurship (IOE), where participants earn a certificate in Entrepreneurship after three months of comprehensive training in all aspects of starting and owning a successful competitive business. The main goal and purpose of IOE is that each year one of the trained businesses will be awarded

## About the Author

up to $10,000 start up money to ensure financial success. The newly added SAT & PSAT prep courses for children ages 9-19 fuels the potential success of all who walk through the doors of New Zion Christian Church.

Apostle Pleasant has met with political officials such as President Clinton and Nelson Mandela. He has delivered the opening prayer for the born again Christian and comedian, Steve Harvey. He has performed marriage ceremonies and counseled numerous celebrated personalities such as Usher Raymond (Confessions Recording Artist), Terri Vaughn (Lavita Jenkins on The Steve Harvey Show), and many others.

He is civically engaged as well. After the Columbine High School shooting, he founded the National School Safety Advocacy Association. His latest foundations include the Young Entrepreneurship Program (YEP) and the African American Consumer Economic Rights Inc (AACER).

## *About the Author*

He has authored six books, *Prayers That Open Heaven, Capturing and Keeping the Pastor's Heart, Powerful Prayers That Open Heaven, Advertising Principles: How to Effectively Reach African Americans in the $21^{st}$ Century, Discover a New You: A 21 Day Journey to Uncovering Your Uniqueness and From My Heart To Yours: Love Letters From A Loving Father.*

Apostle Pleasant is the husband of Kimberly Pleasant (whom he loves dearly) and the proud father of three children: Christian, Zion and Nacara.

# FINI

Made in the USA
Charleston, SC
11 January 2015